THINGS TO DO

WHEN YOU'RE ON A LONG TRIP,
WAITING AROUND,
OR JUST PLAIN BORED…

Ways to Enjoy Your Travel or Waiting Time More…
As Well As Stimulate Your Mind

GINI GRAHAM SCOTT, Ph.D.

iUniverse, Inc.
Bloomington

iUniverse books may be ordered through booksellers or by contacting:

iUniverse
1663 Liberty Drive
Bloomington, IN 47403
www.iuniverse.com
1-800-Authors (1-800-288-4677)

ISBN: 978-1-4620-4415-3 (sc)

Printed in the United States of America

iUniverse rev. date: 09/06/2011

CONTENTS

ABOUT THE AUTHOR

Gini Graham Scott has written a series of books on enjoying your work and leisure, including: *Enjoy! 101 Little Things to Do to Add Fun to Your Work Everyday, The Creative Traveler,* and *Fantasy Worlds,* as well as three books on using your powers of visualization, imagination, and creativity: *The Empowered Mind, How to Harness the Creative Force Within You; Mind Power: Picture Your Way to Success*; and *Want It, See It, Get It!*. Also, she has written several humor books, most notably *Do You Look Like Your Dog?* and *I Want to Be a Sturgeon – and Other Wrong Things that Kids Write.*

Aside from these books, she has published over 50 books on various topics, and has gained extensive media interest for previous books, including appearances on *Good Morning America, Oprah, Montel Williams, CNN,* and hundreds of radio interviews.

She has a PhD in Sociology from the University of California at Berkeley, and MAs in Anthropology, Mass Communications and Organizational/Consumer/Audience Behavior, and Popular Culture and Lifestyles at Cal State East Bay. She is now getting an M.S. there in Recreation and Tourism.

INTRODUCTION

Have you gone on a long trip where you have gotten bored while traveling or waiting in an airport or bus or train station? Do you need a quick pick up to help in your job search? Have you wondered how to pass the time and amuse yourself, when you can't use your cell phone, read, or listen to music?

Well, this little book -- *THINGS TO DO WHEN YOU ARE ON A LONG TRIP, WAITING AROUND, OR JUST PLAIN BORED* – is the perfect antidote. It features a variety of fun and creative things you can do in your imagination or by being more perceptive, speaking, or interacting with others. Activities range from interesting things to think about and imagine to mind games to enjoy with yourself and others, and more.

I got the idea for this book while commuting back and forth between Oakland and L.A., since I own a house in Oakland and for two years had an office/apartment in Santa Monica to help me break into the film industry, while also pursuing a career writing books, speaking, and consulting on work relationships. From August 2007 to August 2009, I spent 2-3 weeks a month in each place and drove for about seven hours each way.

While I started out listening to the radio and occasional tapes, I sometimes found myself getting bored and restless. Using a cell phone to have a conversation was distracting and is now illegal unless you use a headphone or Bluetooth.

Thus, as I drove, I began thinking of things to do to make the time go faster and came up with all kinds of ideas. As a result, instead of a slog, these trips turned out to be both relaxing and stimulating excursions which I looked forward to. The long drive became like another vacation trip.

As I tried out different ways of staying alert and amusing myself, I began to write these ideas down or say them aloud into a cassette-recorder. The result was hundreds of different activities that range from building your brain power, charging up your memory, and thinking of how to be more successful at work to just having fun. You can even play mental games and safely give yourself a mini-massage with one hand as you drive. In fact, these activities will help you stay very aware and alert, so you drive even more safely.

While these techniques are ideal for traveling on a long trip, you can apply them in many other situations, such as feeling better while job hunting or waiting for something to happen. Or use them as a great icebreaker or fun activity for a get-together with friends or at a party.

If you are driving while doing these exercises, do them safely. For example, these exercises are best when you are driving on a straight-away, so you don't have to think much about your driving or can use these exercises to help you stay alert and engaged. If you are driving fast, making a lot of turns, or looking for a turnoff, don't do them. Should you have to make a quick maneuver, stop doing whatever you are doing and focus on the road. As long as you are doing straight driving, where you are largely driving on automatic, you are generally safe to do these exercises.

If you have to do something, such as make a turn, plan ahead or take some time out, so you can perform that action without distraction and can focus on being aware of the environment around you. Then, you can return to doing these exercises, once you can focus on them again.

While you can speak aloud or have conversations in your mind as ideas come to you, you can easily record your thoughts and listen back to them later on a small recorder, such as a Bluetooth recorder, about the size of a large flash drive. You can easily set this up with an earpiece or chain around your neck, so you don't have to hold it as you drive or walk someplace. And if you're out in public, it will look more natural if you speak into a recorder rather than talk aloud, which might look odd or crazy, if you seem to be talking to yourself.

I've organized these ideas into several categories in no particular order, so feel free to skip around and pick out those activities that especially appeal to you.

Besides simply having fun with these things to do, you can use many of these techniques to stimulate your mind, work out problems, make decisions, increase your creativity, overcome stress, relax, and more.

As you do these exercises, there may be things you want to remember. If so, write them down on a pad or in a notebook as you think of them – or take some time out at a rest stop to record them. Another approach is to have a recording device with you – one you can clip onto something if you are driving, and speak into it as you come up with ideas. Later you can listen to or transcribe them to refer to them later.

You can do most of these activities with one or more other people. You can share any of the things you are observing, seeing, tasting and imagining, and you can take turns doing the exercises, and sharing your experiences with each other. Or you can interact and build on each other's experiences.

You can come up with more ideas for exercises yourself – or come up with these by sharing your ideas together.

CHAPTER 1: RELAX

- Meditate. Just chant the word "om" aloud or to yourself, focus on a word or sound, experience the stillness of the world around you, or engage in your favorite type of meditation. Just let your mind go, while keeping your eyes open as you relax but stay alert. If someone is in the car with you, you can do this together.

- See how long you can say a sound like "om" as you breathe out. Try experimenting with different sounds, like "weeee"… "ahhhhh"… "oooooh"…. "heeee" ….. "yuuuuuu".

- As you chant or say sounds, notice what images or colors come to mind. Try playing with those images as you chant or say sounds, such as watching the words or images expand as you chant more loudly or watching them vibrate more slowly or quickly as your chants are slower or faster.

- Think of your favorite place to relax, like on a sunny beach, on a mountain top, or a river, and imagine yourself there.

- Give yourself a massage with your free hand as you drive on a long straight away, when you can comfortably drive with one hand. Or use both hands if you are a passenger. You can massage your face, neck, arms, and legs.

- Exercise your neck and other limbs through doing limited stretching, while you are seated behind the wheel or in a chair. For example, move your neck left and right, up and down, and repeat these movements, always coming back to the center. Stretch your right arm up and down several times, while your left hand is on the wheel or resting on your lap; then reverse, so you stretch your left arm in the same manner.

- Put some soothing instrumental music on the radio or listen to it on a player or mobile device. As the music plays, imagine yourself feeling more and more relaxed as well as calm and happy, but still alert and aware, so you continue to listen, but don't drift off to sleep.

- While you relax, add in some triggers to remind yourself to stay alert, such as clicking your fingers together, if you start to become overly relaxed or sleepy.

- Take a break from time to time from getting more and more relaxed, so you still feel comfortable, yet stay alert.

CHAPTER 2: BE HAPPY

- Think of all the things you are grateful for – and review your list anytime you are in or see a traffic jam across the road or are in a crowded room. As you recall everything you feel grateful for, you'll feel better – much better – already.

- Think about your favorite things. Make a list in your mind, and imagine you are with that favorite person, doing that favorite activity, or in that favorite place.

- See yourself surrounded by the people you like.

- Imagine you are with someone you really like being with, and you are doing whatever you like to do best together.

- Recall a time when you were really happy as a little kid, and think about all the fun you had.

- Remember some of your best friends when you were a child at different ages, and recall some of the fun times you had together.

- Remember some of your best friends when you were a teenager in junior high, high school, or college, and recall some of the fun times you had together.

- Remember some of your favorite people from the first or second job you had, and recall some of the times you enjoyed together.

- See yourself surrounded by a glowing white light of happiness, and imagine it caressing you, warming you, and protecting you.

- Remember a favorite joke and tell yourself that joke – either mentally or say it aloud.

- Remember a favorite song – and imagine yourself listening to it or singing it – or sing it aloud.

- Recall a favorite game you liked to play as a child or adult, and imagine yourself playing it now – and of course, you win!

- Imagine yourself getting dressed up in a costume for a party, and see yourself going to the party and having fun.

- Imagine yourself dressed in a favorite outfit and admire yourself in front of a mirror. Then imagine yourself going someplace, where everyone looks at you admiringly or praises you for what you are wearing.

- Imagine yourself going shopping for some fun product or for something to wear. Imagine you see exactly what you want, and you try it out or put it on and admire yourself while in the store.

- Imagine yourself going to an amusement park, and you are having fun seeing the crowds and going on the rides. Imagine yourself doing this as a kid or doing it now.

- Imagine yourself freely running through the meadows, fields, or woods you are passing, and you feel very free, happy, and exhilarated as you run.

- Imagine yourself as one of the animals you see around you, and imagine that you are running around, exploring, and using your senses to experience whatever you are doing more fully.

- Recall a time when you got a reward or praise for something you did, and feel great as you experience being rewarded or praised. You might imagine yourself in front of an individual or group as you get acknowledged and honored for what you did.

- Think about your biggest accomplishments, and make a list of these. Feel a great sense of pride as you think of each one.

CHAPTER 3: WORK IT OUT

- Is there some issue or problem you want to work through? If so, imagine you are a movie director, and see the scene play out with different endings that might help you decide what to do in the actual situation.

- Are you unsure what your goals are? Think about the possible goals you might have, and think about which ones are the most important for you to achieve now.

- Are you going to be doing an interview for something? Imagine yourself doing the interview in your mind, and see yourself doing it very well.

- Is there anyone you want to improve your relationship with or do you want to make amends for something? Imagine what you might do in your mind and think of different alternatives; then decide which one would be the best to do in the actual situation.

- Have you had a conflict with someone? Try visualizing the conflict again, like it is happening now. Then, imagine yourself trying different alternatives to resolve the conflict, such as talking to the person, sending a note about what happened and how you propose to resolve it, or hoping the conflict will go away if you do nothing. Finally, let the outcome of these different alternatives come into your mind without your trying to do anything to shape the result. Now see which outcome you like the best, and try that alternative in the real situation – and good luck. Often your powers of visualization and intuition will tell you what to do.

- If you have had a conflict with someone, imagine different scenarios corresponding to the five ways of resolving conflict – compromise, accommodation, avoidance, collaboration, and confrontation. Imagine what you would do in each situation, like you are a film director seeing a scene play out in your mind. In compromise, you each give a little; in accommodation, you go along with what the other person wants; in avoidance, you delay dealing with the situation or don't do anything about it; in collaboration, you each spend time discussing and working out a resolution; and in confrontation, you decide what you want to do and tell the other person that's how you want to resolve the situation. Then, see what happens in each situation, and decide which outcome you like the best, and try that in the real situation. Commonly, your intuition will give you the best result.

- Is there something you want to change in your life, such as making a change in a relationship, your job, or where you live? Whatever it is, imagine you are going from where you are now to different future possibilities and notice which one feels best for you.

- Has something been going wrong in your life that you want to repair? Think about the different solutions that might be possible, and list the ones that seem to be the best. Then, if you can, make a choice now, or think about what to do later.

- Think about some problems or issues that you recently resolved and notice what you did to resolve them. Then, think about how you might use those resolutions in situations that are unresolved now or might come up in the future.

• Imagine that you are talking to someone who can help you resolve a problem you are experiencing – a friend, counselor, religious leader, teacher, or spiritual or religious guide. After you say the problem aloud, imagine that the person you are speaking to gives you some answers.

• Say you are trying to decide what kind of work to do next. Imagine a triangle in which one edge is your skills; another is the kind of jobs that are most available; the third is your priorities, what you would like to do if you could do anything. Then, think about each side of the triangle. First, list your strongest skills. Second, list the kind of work that is most in demand now. Third, list what you would most liked to do. Then, think about where there is the best fit in the middle of the triangle to see which are the strongest connections between your skills, available jobs, and your preferences. You might imagine lines connecting from one side of the triangle to another and a button that lights up each time you make a connection.

• What do you want to do? What do you like to do? Think back on the jobs that you have had and ask yourself a series of questions. Notice what answers come to you. The questions to ask include these: What has been your favorite job or jobs? What did you like about your favorite jobs? If there were other jobs you didn't like, what didn't you like about them? What skills did you use in these jobs you most like using? Which did you like using the least? You can use these answers to help you decide what kind of job you want to do next and what skills you have to bring to the job.

• Think about the kinds of skills you used and most like using in different situations. Go back into your past and recall how you developed or used these skills as a little kid or teenager. Notice if there were certain activities you were especially drawn to. Reflecting back can help you decide what you most want to do and are good at doing today.

- As you pass a series of mile markers or see a clock's hand move from minute to minute or pass each five minutes marker, think of that as a year or 5 year period in your life from your childhood to the present. Then, think of a significant or memorable event associated with that time period or milestone. Keep doing this by decade or for the sweep of your life, and notice any patterns in the milestones that occurred. Do they tend to be family milestones, work milestones, or a combination of these? These patterns can help you clarify who you are, where you are going, and the next series of milestones along the way.

- Think of the milestones in your life going backwards or forwards. Imagine each of them marked by a milepost. If you are going backwards, you can use these milestones to help you understand how you got to where you are now.

  - For example, if you are reflecting on a relationship, you might go back as far as you can for the first significant event that happened in your relationship, such as meeting someone, going on a first date, proposing, or getting married. Focus first on the really positive and pleasant experiences. Then, if any negative things happened, think of them as learning experiences and think how you might use that experience to improve things in the future – in a current relationship or in a future one.

  - If you are a parent, think about the highlights that were really good and the things that were troublesome in raising your child. Then, think about how you might make changes or do things differently.

- Or think about your milestones at work, from getting your first job to the one you have now. What were the highlights that were really good? What things were really difficult? And how might you make changes or do things differently as a result?

- Now try remembering back to when you were a little kid or teenager. Notice if there were things you were especially drawn to; recall what you most liked to do. This way you create a map or timeline of the early milestones that stand out for you. Then, think about what you are doing now, and if you are doing those things you were especially drawn to or liked the most as a young kid. Or is there anything you really liked that you aren't doing now? Maybe this might be something to bring back into your life now, since you liked it so much at one time.

CHAPTER 4: IMAGINE IT

- Imagine that imaginary creatures are walking across the land. See one or more of them emerge out of a field, grove of trees, or from a building, and imagine them walking or running in the distance. Then, ask yourself questions to add a story or details to your fantasy, such as: "Where is it going?," "What is it going to do?," "Why is it going there?," "Who is with?" and so on.

- Imagine the world around you in different colors. For instance, imagine what the landscape would look like if you took a brush and painted it different colors, such as pink for the sky, purple of the grass, blue for the trees. Let your color palate go wild, as you paint the scene in your mind. Or imagine the room you are in has a new color scheme.

- Imagine that you see someone walking in the distance. In your mind's eye, notice what that person is like, what he might do, where he is going. You might also imagine that you pick this person up in your car or he or she comes over to where you are waiting. Then, have an imaginary conversation with that person.

- Imagine the landscape you are passing or room where you are is part of a video game. You see characters, like warriors, lions, tigers, dinosaurs, or imaginary creatures, appear and fight it out. Imagine that you are shooting pellets at them, and each time you make a hit, the character falls over. Or if you miss your target, too bad. You can always shoot again.

• Imagine you are seeing or writing down graffiti when you pass a wall. Think about what you would write, and see the words or drawings appear there.

• Imagine you are young child, seeing everything you pass from the eyes of a child. What do you notice that's fun and exciting?

• Imagine that you are walking around in the places you are passing or down the corridors of a building where you are. Project yourself into the scene and see yourself walking in the fields, on the streets, in the mountains; or enter a luxury suite, a lively nightclub, or a fancy party. Go wherever you want to go in your imagination.

• Notice the people who are walking by or passing you in cars. Imagine who they are and where they are going. Create a little story about how they are related to each other and what they are doing.

• As people pass by or you pass them, imagine they are dressed differently than they are; imagine they are in a different kind of car. For example, if people are dressed casually, say for a camping trip, imagine them dressed to the nines for a fancy party. If people are driving in a sleek sports car, imagine they are driving an old clunker. You can likewise change the colors of what they are wearing or the car they are driving.

• Imaging you are looking at a scene from a different perspective. For example, as you look at the landscape from your car, imagine that you are in an airplane flying above the landscape, and notice what you see.

- Notice the birds above you – or imagine they are flying above you. Then, imagine you are one of those birds and experience flying as that bird. Feel the wind rush by and the landscape pass quickly before you as you race through the air. Imagine you are zooming up and down, flying fast and then slow. Now imagine that you are looking around as that bird – you might see clouds, other birds around you. Then, look down on the ground and notice the landscape move and change under you as you fly.

- As you drive or walk along, you may notice some bugs fly by. You might brush some away if they come close – or some may just zoom past, and a few go splat. Now imagine what it would be like to experience the world as a bug. Imagine yourself flying low to the ground and seeing everything around you from the insect's point of view. First, you're skittering around looking at the flowers and leaves. Then, you see other bugs fly by. Perhaps follow some of them and see where they go. Also notice how you may have to fly even faster to protect yourself, such as from a bird looking for its next meal. Or perhaps you notice the silky strands of a spider web ahead, and you dip down to elude it. So go ahead, be a bug and imagine what you see as you fly around – and be careful not to crash into anything and go splat.

- As you drive or walk on the city streets, notice the power lines around you. Imagine you are climbing up and down these power lines, perhaps as a repair person or as someone who is curious and wants to look around. Or perhaps imagine yourself as a bird perching on the wires and looking down on the fields or city below.

- As you look ahead to the end of a road or path, imagine where it is going and imagine yourself going along the road or path to someplace special. Perhaps it is a vacation spot such as a beach, where you see people sitting or eating under their umbrellas. Maybe some people are sunning themselves or putting on suntan lotion. Then, the scene becomes more dramatic. For example, people start tilting umbrellas at each other. Someone runs by and sends sand flying at the people sunning themselves, and they give chase. Or imagine an even more fantastical scene, such as a magic castle at the end of the road with ivory walls that glisten in the sun. Whatever you see, imagine yourself going there and enjoying the experience. Perhaps imagine yourself like royalty going to visit your castle and forest with game. No matter where you are, imagine yourself going to the end of a road or a path, and see what you discover at the end.

• As you pass trucks on the road or see them on the street, think about what the trucks are carrying. Sometimes it's clear, because there is a name of a supermarket, manufacturer, or type of produce listed on the side of the truck; or if not, imagine what might be in that truck. Maybe it's just boxes, produce, or other everyday objects. But as you let your imagination go, you may see other things in there, such as hidden treasure, someone hiding in the back of the truck, maybe some animals. Or maybe the truck has a trailer attached. You can create stories about what is in that truck and where is it going – maybe it's just going to drop off what it is carrying, but maybe other things might happen to it along the way from a blow-out to getting hijacked or being pulled into a UFO by aliens. Or if there are animals or a horse trailer, you could name the animals or horses and write stories about them, such as if they in a circus or are on their way to perform on a movie set.

• As different trucks pass by, you might imagine who the truck driver is, where he comes from, and what he thinks about driving a truck. For example, is he a tough New Yorker, a feisty redneck, an ex-military soldier, a college student driving a truck for kicks on weekends? Also, imagine what the driver might look like, if you can't see into the cab. For instance, one driver could have a bushy mustache, another just out of the army could have a buzz cut. You might imagine the background of the truck driver, what his family is like, and how he feels about going on a long trip. You could image what it would be like to be a truck driver, what you would like to drive in your truck, and where you might go as you travel to different cities.

- Try imagining funny things that happen to the trucks or cars of people who pass by. For example, what if a jack rabbit suddenly darted out in front of the truck. The truck driver might have to stop on the spot. But luckily a woman in a sports car drives by, and she has a jack, so he can fix his wheels. Then, he drives off – or does he? Maybe he is so taken by the woman in the sports car that he offers her a ride, and love develops from there. But then you might imagine little twists and turns in the story, such as suppose he has another flat or gets stopped by bandits? Suppose he and the woman discover they know someone in common, and she once had a relationship with one of his close friends? Just suppose. Suppose. Anything becomes possible. Try letting the story tell itself and you follow-along like one of the listeners, not sure where the story is going next, and entranced and eager to follow it as a result.

- You might notice people who are in different occupations, reflected in the way they look or dress. Then, imagine yourself as someone in that occupation. For instance, say someone looks thin and athletic like a dancer. Imagine yourself as a dancer and imagine the kind of dance you would perform and the kind of music you would dance to. Then, see yourself sailing across the dance floor as a lone performer or as part of a team. You might imagine the audience in the stands watching you and cheering you on.

Or imagine yourself as a skater jumping and pirouetting all over the ice.

• You might imagine stories about the cars you notice passing by. For example, maybe one man is driving quickly because his wife is having a baby, and they want to rush to the hospital. Or maybe someone is going by at 100 miles per hour because he loves the experience of racing and wants to drive as fast as he can. Still another person is racing to get where she is going very quickly, such as to an important business meeting. Others are just in the habit of driving quickly. So think about these different scenarios for the people you see around you, and ask yourself who they are, where they are going, and why. Then, imagine what happens when they get to wherever they are going.

• As you listen to music, imagine scenes you might see in front of you as the director of a movie, musical, or opera. Let the music suggest images, scenes, and stories to you, and in your mind's eye, see people performing or engaging in the activities the music suggests. For instance, a lyrical, fully orchestrated piece might suggest people going out into the fields or dancing by a stream. If you have a strong visual sense, even with your eyes open, you can see these scenes in front of you.

• If it is dark, you might see people, animals, or other beings enacting scenes in the sky, much like the ancients used to visualize gods in the sky associated with a constellation. You might imagine the art associated with different constellations or create your own. You might see creatures or some of the traditional Greek or Roman gods, such as Neptune or Mercury, sitting regally in the sky. Or perhaps see images associated with the different constellations, such as the hunter Orion chasing a rabbit or deer.

- Or if it is light, imagine people from the sky coming down to earth and walking across the fields, hills, or other places you pass. You could see these sky being as ordinary people who have parachuted to earth, or they could be large giants, or even aliens arriving in a spaceship.

- You might imagine action scenes played out by some well-known actors, especially those who have been in action movies, such as Brad Pitt, Keanu Reeves, Clive Owen, Nicholas Cage, or Angela Jolie. Imagine they are in an adventure, such as racing across the fields. Or maybe you see a superhero like Superman or Ironman appear in your story. It's like you have cast your own movie to direct, and you see your action-adventure movie play out in the countryside or streets around you.

- Create your own avatar and join the action you are imagining, much like creating an avatar for video game, so in your imagination, you could chase or be chased by the bad guys in your movie or game.

- If you are with a friend or friends, try building on each others stories. The process is similar to what happens when one person starts a story and the other person continues it. Or consider the process like brainstorming, where you each let your mind go and think of whatever comes to mind to continue the story, no matter how outrageous or silly it may be.

- Try thinking of driving in a car or walking from place to place as you pass signs along the way like a ship traveling from port to port. Try imagining that each port represents a different memorable experience in your life or a particular place or destination, and you go to different ports as you drive or walk along. As you do, imagine the different fun things you do there. Or try projecting yourself into someone else as you do this. For instance, imagine you're a sailor or a tourist on cruise ship, and you stop at different ports, get off, and look around. So what do you see as a sailor? As a tourist? Maybe you could go to some nightclubs or bars. Maybe you could stop at a shop and purchase some souvenirs. Just let your imagination go, and have fun going where you want. Then, return to the ship and go on to the next port.

- Besides exploring the ports where you stop, you can imagine the ship as a place to have fun and imagine the activities you might engage in there. For instance, you might play volleyball or badminton, go dancing, have dinner with the captain. Or maybe you meet somebody really interesting to talk to. Again, let your imagination roam freely and experience whatever comes to you.

CHAPTER 5: FOOD FOR THOUGHT

- Say you're feeling hungry as you're driving along or waiting somewhere, but don't have a chance to get some food right away. This is a perfect time to imagine the kind of meal you are going to have – or would like to have. You might image the plate in front of you or a waitress bringing it to you. You could image a chef cooking your meal in the kitchen. As you think about, see the plate with the food in your mind's eye and smell it. Imagine you are eating it and taste it in your imagination. Good, huh? You may find you aren't hungry after doing this – you have finished your meal in your mind's eye.

- Imagine you are having a cool drink and it tastes really good. Imagine yourself drinking it very slowly, so you can enjoy the coolness and notice its taste, whether it's sweet or sour, smooth or fizzy, or has a mild or tangy taste. As you visualize your drink, imagine you are swishing it around in your mouth, really enjoying it.

- Now as you drive or walk towards your next stop, imagine what kinds of food will be on the menu. Imagine you are choosing whatever you want from a lavish buffet. See yourself putting whatever you have chosen on a plate, and move it close to you, so you can smell, taste, and touch all the food that's on it.

- Imagine you have a chicken leg, turkey wing, barbecue beef rib, or other food item you can pick up in front of you. Notice how it smells as you pick it up. Experience touching it and feeling its texture. Notice if it's soft or slick, or if the skin is tough or crispy. Imagine running your fingers across whatever you are going to eat and feel how warm it is. Notice how it goes from hot to warm to cool as you continue to hold it. Then, imagine yourself eating it and feel it warming up your body as you eat.

- Try imagining where the food you are eating – in reality or in your imagination – came from. See it being created from the ground up.

  - For example, say you've ordered a hamburger. You might see it being created in a factory, where it is ground up and put into patties. Or maybe see the cows that are contributing their meat to this hamburger. You might see them grazing on a grassy field and then led through a chute into the factory. Or to go back even further, imagine the grass growing from seed in the ground before the cows eat it.

  - Or say you are a vegetarian. You might have a plate of vegetables in front of you or image they are there. Think about how these vegetables got cooked and before that how they were grown. Or perhaps imagine a truck taking the vegetables to a produce plant, where they cut up the vegetables or squeeze them to take out their juice.

- Think about how nutritious the food you are eating is. Imagine how each of the nutritious elements in your food has its own character, like a superhero. For example, a strong guy in tights who has bulging muscles and a big chest is Vitamin B; a thin gangly man with carrot orange hair and glasses is Vitamin A; a woman with an outfit like

Wonder Woman with yellow sunbursts is Vitamin D; and so on. Imagine these characters are gathered around you as you eat good food, cheering you on, so you really are eager to eat it, even if you haven't been interested in that food in the past. Later, after you visualize eating good food in this way, you will find you are more drawn to actually eat it in everyday life.

• Imagine that you are a little kid again, and you're eating your vegetables. Imagine you are tasting them, counting them, moving them around, and playing with them on your plate. Imagine you are using your fingers to feel them, as you put them in your mouth and taste them. Perhaps imagine your parents sitting nearby; at first they don't notice you, but when they do, maybe they tell you not to play with your food or send you to your room. But then, you can use going to your room as an opportunity to play with your food and have fun with it, such as creating lakes in the mashed potatoes, imagining the celery stalks are like swords, or piling up the peas as high as you can. Just see yourself enjoying this food play, as you do whatever you want in your mind's eye.

• If you are trying to diet and are hungry, imagine that you are holding a candy bar – or even hold a real candy bar. But don't open the package and don't eat it. Then, in your mind or in reality, touch the candy bar, feel it, stroke it, massage it, imagine yourself tasting it in your mind. If you've eaten this candy bar before, you know what it would taste like. Imagine yourself smelling it and moving it around in your mouth and chewing it. Just fully experience the sensation of eating the candy bar without actually eating it. The experience could be a way to actually reduce your weight, because the visualization takes the place of eating the candy bar. And if you get hungry again later, try experiencing and "eating" another virtual candy bar.

- Is there any other food you really like? As with the virtual candy bar, imagine that food on a plate in front of you, and you not only see it, but touch it, smell it, and taste it in your mind's eye. As you do, notice the food's textures and whether it is smooth or crunchy as you chew it in your imagination. Just think of all the calories you won't consume, as you experience enjoying your food in your mind's eye.

CHAPTER 6: SEE IT

- Be a birdwatcher. Watch for birds flying by and see if you can identify them. Count the number of each type of bird that flies by. Notice where they go and what they do.

- Glance at the clouds ahead and notice what you see in them. See if you can observe a person's face, an animal, a house or castle, a fountain, a river. Then, notice how those shapes change as you ride along or look back at the clouds from time to time.

- Count cows, dog, or other animals. See how many you count as you drive or walk by.

- Pay attention to the way the terrain changes as you travel along. Notice if the changes are gradual or sudden. Notice if there are fences separating the different terrains. Notices how the colors change, as you move from place to place, like the colors on a painter's palate.

- Notice certain colors. Pick an unusual color, like red or silver for cars if you are driving, pink or purple for jackets or handbags if you are in a waiting room, and see how many go by. When they do, engage in some kind of fun ritual or response, such as thinking or calling out the color and name of what you see, such as: "Red car!" or "Pink jacket" – or any name you associate with that color, such as: "Silver Bullet!"

- Imagine you are a camera, and imagine you are framing pictures as you drive or walk along. Click the shutter whenever you see a picture you like and want to remember it.

- Imagine you are a private eye investigating something, and you are looking for something special in your investigation. For instance, imagine you are looking for a car of a certain color or with a license plate from a nearby state. Or maybe you are looking for cars with three or more people in them or noticing how often trucks pass. You might look for call boxes along the road. Just pick something less common or unusual to look for and see how often you see it.

- Imagine you have to give someone a report of what you have just seen, such as a passing train, large house, group of people on a street corner, or something else that has caught your eye. You have only a few seconds to look at it, but do so as attentively as you can to remember it. Then, report what you have seen, either in your mind's eye or by speaking aloud to someone – and if you are with someone, you can do this with each other.

- Imagine that someone will question you on what you have seen, like you are a witness on the stand. So as you drive or walk along, notice as much as you can, such as the writing and images on signs on the road or buildings. Then, stop along the side of the road or pause whatever you are doing, and see how much you can remember and describe. If you have looked very closely, you should be able to spend more time describing than you spent looking at something. After you have finished your description, look back at what you described, and see how accurate you were.

- Look for bumper stickers on cars or statements on T-shirts or buttons and notice what they say. If they suggest any pictures, imagine them in your mind's eye. Or if they state an idea or opinion, speak back to agree or disagree – in your imagination or by speaking your thoughts aloud.

- Pick a color and notice things of that color. Next look for things of two colors, and see how often those two colors turn up. For example, say you choose green and brown. As you pass a field, you might notice the green grass and bushes surrounding a field of brownish wheat.

- As cars or people pass by, imagine you are seeing the world from their point of view. For example, imagine you are looking at a landscape from the perspective of people in another car; imagine that you are looking at the city streets around you from the vantage point of someone walking down the street. Or imagine yourself as one of the people passing by who is looking at you.

- Try imagining you are a bird, like an owl, and you can see very far. Look around, as if you are that owl, and see how far you can see. If you see something that might cover or hide something else, such as the door to a house or some thick bushes, imagine what you might find there. For instance, maybe some object is hidden in the bushes, such as a treasure box or piece of jewelry. Imagine that you have X-ray vision, so you can see through doors and bushes, and imagine what's there.

- When it's dark and you are driving, notice the lights around you. See how far they extend, indicating the size of whatever's there. Estimate how many lights there are. Try imagining what the area might be like during the day.

- When it's early evening, you might look into the sky to see the moon or the beginning of the stars in the sky. Glance at them from time to time, and notice how their position changes in the sky.

- If the sun is just setting, be aware of the colors as it goes down. Notice that it's darker towards the horizon, and as you glance up in the sky, notice how it gets more gray and pink, which fades into blue and then becomes an even darker blue as you look higher into the sky. Notice how the colors of the sky change as you glance up from time to time, as it gets darker and darker.

- Notice how the sun or moon moves in the sky as you drive. If it is during the day, notice how the shadows change in size and direction. If it is night, notice how the moon rises higher or lower in the sky, and how it changes size from being larger when it is closer to the horizon to smaller as it climbs higher in the sky.

- Try doing some exercises to increase your visual acuity and stimulate and strengthen your eyes. Some people with glasses use this technique and find they need their glasses less or not at all. If you are driving, do these techniques quickly and continually refocus back on the road before doing the exercise again. Here are a few of these exercises:

  - Imagine a clock, where you look around to each number and bring your eyes back so you look straight ahead for each numbers. For example, look up to where the number "12" is, and then back to center. Look at where the number "1" is, and back to center. Keep doing this exercise in a clockwise direction, and afterwards repeat in a counterclockwise direction.

  - Look at something close to you, such as your hand on the steering wheel, and then look at something far away, such as the road ahead. Switch back and forth between looking at something close and at something far away. Or try moving one of your fingers back and forth, as you focus on it first very close and then very far away.

- Alternate looking at things that are both far and near on the road to stimulate your eye muscles. For example, look to your right at the plants on the side of the road, to your left at the cars passing you, and look straight ahead to see cars in front of you and as far as you can see ahead down the road. Then, go back to looking at the bushes and at any cars passing you, and return to look straight ahead. Continue to do this exercise for several minutes, moving from one position to another – straight ahead, 30 to 45 degrees to the right, 30 to 45 degrees to the left. Just keep shifting where you are looking from one position to another.

- Look as far as you can to either side and return your eyes to center. Repeat this exercise for a few minutes. This will strengthen your peripheral vision.

- Try squinting to see things even more clearly, since squinting narrows your field of vision, so things that may initially seem fuzzy become less so. For example, if you are looking ahead in the darkness, the lights ahead may seem to expand like the rays of the sun. But when you squint, the lights become smaller and sharper. Likewise, if the lettering on a sign ahead looks a little blurry, squinting will make it sharper. Squinting and unsquinting repeatedly will help strengthen your eyes, too.

CHAPTER 7: BE CREATIVE

- Think about some creative project you want to do – such as a writing a book, painting a picture, writing a song, or whatever. Then, work out what you want to do in your mind.

- Write your memoirs in your mind. Pick a day and imagine you are writing about it. See it as vividly as you can in your mind's eye.

- Create a fantasy story that takes place on the landscape you are passing or in the room where you are waiting. For example, imagine some aliens landing outside your car or walking through the door; imagine a rocket ship launching on a field or outside your window. Then, imagine what happens next. Are the aliens friendly? Do they come over to talk to you? Or maybe you just see a friend or relative who has become a playful cat. Let your imagination fly, and you'll find that time flies, too.

- Create a story or drama sparked by whatever you see around you. Say you are passing a stand of fruit trees. You might imagine a chase through them, as one person runs after the other. Or maybe someone is trying to bury someone or something there. Perhaps someone has a necklace or box of treasures they want to hide. Or say you pass some electric poles. You might imagine someone trying to climb up one of the poles to get away from someone chasing him and now he is cornered. So what happens? Maybe he gets trapped up there or gets electrocuted. Maybe he escapes. Or suppose you see clusters of trees. Maybe those could be hiding places, such as for the person who escaped from the electric pole. Just let your imagination go free, as you drive or walk along and see things that trigger your imagination. Incorporate whatever you see into your imaginary story.

- Try stringing whatever you see into a continuing story, which could even turn into a script, novel, or memoir. Write them down or record them as you observe or soon afterwards, so you remember.

  o For example, say you're passing a field, where some crops are growing. You might imagine a farmer watering the terrain and some people helping him. If you are politically inclined, you might think about where these field workers come from and their living conditions. Are they immigrant laborers? Do they have visas or green cards? Have they been illegally brought here? If so, you might imagine some cars coming towards the field, and the workers see them. As the cars come closer, they look like police cars, and the workers start running as fast as they can, while the police run after them.

  o Alternatively, maybe the farmer works with his workers, and after a hard day, he goes into his house where he sees his family with lots of kids. Then, they all gather for dinner, when the phone rings, and he hears an important message that changes everything. So what happens now?

- Whatever the scenario, let your imagination flow freely and let the story come to you. Later, you can decide what to do with it, if you want to turn it into a script or novel. Think of yourself as a free flowing fountain, with ideas pouring out. Later you can guide that water into a channel which you can direct anywhere, and the stream of water becomes more and more powerful as the water streams through faster and faster. Likewise, the ideas flowing through your mind can be very powerful, as you gather and channel them into a script, novel, or other projects. But first you need the water flowing freely so you can gather it. So let it flow.

- Think of children's stories from your childhood and imagine how you might change them. For example, take Goldilocks and the three bears. Instead of having three bears, maybe she meets three horses. Goldilocks starts talking to the horses and getting to know them. She imagines herself like a horse and sees herself transforming into a horse. Next, she begins prancing around and enjoys what it feels like to be a horse. Then, she hears a voice, and it's her parents calling her. She can't go out to see them, because she's a horse, so she tells them she's in the barn, and when they ask why, she says she's feeding the horses, but doesn't tell them she has become a horse. But then a good witch appears and turns her back into a person, and now when she looks at the horses, she feels a shared understanding, because she knows what it's like to be a horse. So now, you try transforming some classic children's stories to make them your own.

- You might imagine you are writing a kid's picture book and incorporate things you see as you drive, walk along, or wait for something. Or perhaps imagine you are that kid telling that story. For instance, say you imagine you are a little kid on a boring trip with his parents, and you start to imagine all sorts of amazing things that happen on the trip, such as cars that take off and fly and magical characters that appear on the road and invite you into the forest to experience new adventures.

- Or imagine writing a kid's picture book about the interesting people you meet or observe. Think what a kid might be experiencing – or how you might have experienced those people as young child. For example, say you are stopped at a gas station, when a truck pulls in, and the truck driver steps out. Or perhaps it's a van with colorful characters dressed in unusual clothing, such as long robes. In either case, the kid is surprised, because the truck driver or unusual-looking characters are different from the everyday people the kid usually sees. Then, the driver or character comes over to the kid, and they talk to each other. So the book describes how they get acquainted with and learn about each other; it's a book about understanding and accepting differences. So you see how easy it is – just about anything can stimulate your creativity – and you might later turn it into a published book.

- Now imagine you are writing a novel. Think of the main characters – pick the first characters that come into your mind. Decide what year this is – the present or some time in the past. Consider what these characters are like. Are they rich, poor? Well educated or not? What kind of jobs do they have? How are they are dressed? Where are they living? Take whatever answers come to you. Now think of the first scene when two or more of the main characters are talking to each other. Consider what they are talking about. Maybe they are talking about their daily lives and what happened that day. Or maybe something major happened, such as an earthquake, flood, or serious crime, and they are talking about that. Then, think about what will happen to them as a result of their experiences that day or due to that major event? So now you've got your novel started. Keep going and let the characters live their lives and interact with each other in your mind's eye. As you let your imagination go, you may find that the novel will start to write itself. At some point, record what you have come up with – or describe it as you go along on a cassette or mobile recorder. Later, you can revise and polish what you have written. See! It's easy to be creative and create your own novel in this way.

CHAPTER 8: IT'S A GAME

- You can play all sorts of games in your mind, when you are driving, sitting around, or waiting somewhere. For example, try making estimates about different things and see if they occur – or assess how close your estimate is after something does occur. This technique can improve your ability to make accurate estimates or predictions. For example, while driving, you might estimate whether and when the person in the car behind you will pass you or not – and as necessary move over, so when the person does pass, it's perfectly safe.

- You might create guessing games about whatever's around you. For instance, you might guess how long before you get to the next exit or gas station, and see how close you are. You might guess how long it will be between one sign and the next. You might guess how many seconds or tenths of a mile to get to a distant road crossing the highway. Or try guessing one or two of the letters on the license plate on the next car to pass you. Whenever your guess, see how close you came and notice how you use information or cues around you to determine how to make your guess, such as being aware of your speed and your perception of distance between one thing and another. Or guess how many people are going faster than you and how many seconds before they pass you. If others are in the car with you, you might each venture a guess and see who is closest. Similarly, if you are seated somewhere, you might guess how long it will take a person passing by to walk from one point to another, and compare your guesses with others to see who is the closest.

- Look for something that you see only occasionally. Play a kind of "Where's Waldo" game as you look around by yourself or with others. For instance, if you are driving, you might choose a red car, a hawk, or ivy growing up a tree or a wall. If you are waiting in a busy place, you might choose a woman with red hair, a man with a briefcase. Every time you see one of these chosen items, call out "See it," and if you are doing this with others, score a point for being the first one to spot the object. Then, choose another item and look again.

- Try inventing a game you might play later, such as a board or card game. For example, as you drive or wait for something, think about what you might include in the game, such as a landscape with drawings of trees on a board. Then, think about what equipment you might use (perhaps some things are already around you) and what the rules of play might be. (For example, you throw stones and your goal is to get your stone closest to a series of objects you designate as targets).

- Try playing license bingo while you are driving or waiting someplace where cars drive by. To play, imagine you are looking for two, three, or four numbers, depending on how good you are at remembering them. Then, look for those numbers individually or in combination, and score double or triple if you see those numbers on a license plate together. Whenever you see a number or combination, call it out, and you score for that, and anyone who later sees that number or combination scores, too, but not as much. Or to make the game even harder, you have to see at least two of the chosen numbers on a license plate to score. For example, say I'm looking for a 1, 4, and 7. If I find a 4 on one car, but no 1 or 7, I have to keep looking. Then, the first person to get all the numbers scores a bingo, plus any extra points, such as for finding combinations. Or if you are playing license bingo alone, see how long it takes you to score. Besides being fun, this game is a way to expand your mental abilities, by stimulating your brain to be active as you search for numbers. If you are driving while doing this, keep it safe. For example, as you get close enough to see the license plate of a car in the next lane, speed up or slow down, so you travel at the same speed as the car you are observing. Or if a car is getting ready to pass you, you can slow down and check out their license plate as they pass.

- As a variation on looking for numbers, try letter bingo. In this case, look for letters on license plates or on the signs that you pass. If you are playing with someone else, the first person to spot a letter gets that, though another person could get that same letter if they see it on another license plate or sign. The goal is to see how quickly you can find all the letters or be the first person to find all of them.

CHAPTER 9: SAY WHAT?

- Have a debate with yourself where you take one position and another voice in your head takes another position. Then, debate some topic of interest and imagine the conversation back and forth in your mind, or speak your opinions and ideas aloud. If you wish, choose a winner and imagine you are giving the winner a special award.

- Ask yourself questions – and get answers. Start by picking a topic, any topic. Then, ask yourself questions mentally or aloud – and answer like you are interviewing yourself on radio or TV or having a conversation with yourself. After you ask your question, say whatever comes into your mind. Do this just for fun with wild and wacky questions and answers – or make it serious, and you may get some good answers to important questions you haven't asked or answered before.

- Imagine you are doing an interview with someone -- a real person, imaginary person, celebrity, famous politician, whoever you want to talk to. Imagine a mike between you as you ask questions and let the answers come to you. Or imagine you are putting on the head of the person you are interviewing, and answer as that person as you ask questions.

- Imagine you are a news reporter or announcer describing whatever you see around you – either by speaking aloud or imagining you are doing so. For example, if you are driving, describe the landscape you are passing; if you are walking along a street, describe the buildings and people you pass. Also, notice any activities going on, such as people working or talking in a group. Or imagine some event is going on and describe it as you speak aloud or in your mind.

- Imagine you are a politician giving a speech, and you are trying to convince others of your position and to vote for you. You might be in a studio audience talking to a large audience of listeners and viewers; or you might be addressing a large crowd, as you prefer. In either case, you imagine that everyone is listening carefully to what you are saying and nodding in agreement or cheering you on.

- Imagine you are a teacher explaining something to a class. You might try explaining what you see as you pass by, such as why the clouds gather and move in the sky or why the birds fly in a V. Or perhaps comment on some news you have recently heard on the radio. Whatever it is, explain it aloud or in your mind, and imagine a class of any age – from little kids to college students – listening raptly, intrigued by what you have to say. Then, at the end you might stop for questions and answer them, just as you might if you were a real teacher in a real class.

- Imagine you are a salesperson, trying to sell someone something. It could be a real product or service or something you see around you. For example, as you pass a grove of trees, you might imagine yourself trying to sell those trees to a company rep who buys lumber; as you pass a beautiful house, you might imagine yourself as a real estate agent trying to sell that house; as you pass a store that sells furniture, you might imagine yourself in that store trying to sell a customer a dresser or bed. Whatever you want to sell, imagine yourself selling it. Decide what you want to pitch, and see yourself making the sale.

CHAPTER 10: BUILD YOUR BRAIN

- Do some simple math problems in your head – a great way to stimulate your thinking cap. Start with some easy problems – then make them more difficult to add more of a challenge. For example, add two 3-digit numbers; then go to two numbers with 4-digits. Or try adding two or three numbers with 3 or 4 digits in your head. Or try subtracting one number from another, or multiply or divide some numbers. As you do this, see the calculations like they are on a blackboard or sheet of paper in your mind, Afterwards, check your results. You'll find you'll get better and better with practice.

- Read the signs you observe backwards. For example, a "Stop" sign becomes "Pots," "Belmont" road becomes "Tnomleb." See how quickly you can do this backwards reading. It's a fun mental exercise to stretch your brain.

- Try to remember in sequence as many of the road signs you pass, as in the icebreaker introductions game. You say the name of the last person you met, and then you repeat in sequence all of the other names, such as: "Tom….Janet, Allen, Henry, Tom" and next: "Paul…Tom, Janet, Allen, Henry, Paul." Now do the same with the road signs, saying aloud or mentally the name of the last road you passed, followed by the sequence of any previous signs you passed when you started the challenge.

- Imagine you are adding deposits and subtracting checks in a checkbook. Start with any balance you want. Then, as you imagine you are writing checks, fill out the name of the party to whom you are giving the check and what you have purchased with that check to make it seem more real. Now, mentally deduct that amount in your head. To make a deposit, imagine who has given you that money and imagine you are depositing it in the bank's teller machine. Afterwards, mentally add that amount in your head. As you go through the process, see the balance go up with deposits, down with checks. To make the process easier, start with small checks and round them off, so you don't have to add and subtract any cents, such as adding and subtracting checks for $1, $2, $5, $10, $15, and $25. Once you feel comfortable with such checks, make the process a little harder by adding one decimal point, such as having checks for $1.10; $2.30; $5.20 and so on. Next, go to two decimal places or larger checks, such as $1.25; $2.37; $5.94 or $12.10, $15.20; $15.90. After that try both larger checks and two decimal points. In other words, gradually increase the difficulty of the amounts you are adding or subtracting. This exercise is great for building your concentration, as well as your ability to work with numbers in your head.

- When you see a sign for the next exit, estimate how many minutes it will take you to get there. You can estimate this for the speed you are going, as well as estimate it for going at different speeds. For example, if the next exit is 20 miles away and you are traveling at 60 miles an hour, it should take you 20 minutes. But what if you were going 65 or 70? Try calculating the different times based on different speeds – and whatever your speed, that'll make getting there seem even faster.

CHAPTER 11: GUESS WHAT?

- Guess the miles when you drive, such as to a landmark you see ahead. Look at your odometer before and after you get there, and see how good your guess was. Or guess how long you will have to wait for something to occur and check your watch when this happens. Meanwhile, use other exercises to pass the time.

- Guess how long it'll take to get somewhere as you travel. Pick something in the distance and guess how many minutes it will take you to pass or get to that place. If you making these guesses with others in the car, the winner is whoever comes closest.

- Guess how many people are in the next car you pass or that passes you – or guess the number of people who will come through a door in 1 or 2 minutes. See how many times you are correct or who is correct the most times, if you try this exercise with others.

- Guess whether the next driver of a car or the next person through the door will be male or female. If you try this game with others, see who is correct the most times.

- Estimate how far you have gone, without looking at the odometer. For example, if you have just gotten some gas for the car, think about your driving from the previous destination and imagine how many miles you have traveled.

You'll find that your accuracy will increase as you do this exercise repeatedly, and you will have a much better sense of how fast you are going. You will often find that you have gone much further than you thought, because you have made your trip so much more interesting. This exercise will also increase your ability to sense time and judge the speed at which you are traveling, since you are getting this sense of knowing about how fast you are going and how far you have gone holistically, rather than analytically, using the intuitive part of your brain.

- Try guessing at the number of something you see in front of you when you are stopped or waiting somewhere – such as boxes in a pile, cows in a field, apples on a tree, flowers in a garden. However, rather than trying to count every object in your mind, try snapping a picture of what you are looking at, like you are a camera. Then, call up the picture, and count the number of objects in it. Afterwards, you can look back at the scene that inspired your picture to see how close you were With practice, you will get better and better at taking clear pictures, being able to look at them closely, and get an accurate count.

CHAPTER 12: MAKING PLANS

- Create a to-do list. Think of all the things you need to do and create your top 7 or top 10 list. Record your to-do list on a CD or digital recorder, or later write these things down. Imagine yourself doing these tasks and think about what you need to do to get them done.

- Think about an event you might plan – an imaginary event or a real one you would like to organize if you had the time and money. Imagine what you might do at this event, the activities you might have, the food you might serve, the people you might invite.

- Try planning a wedding just for fun.

  - Imagine what it would be like if it was a small wedding, just for family and close friends. Imagine what you would have to do to prepare for it; imagine the invitations you would send; the gifts you would get; the decorations for the event. Notice where it is being held and who is conducting the service. Image what the bride and groom might say in their vows. Finally, imagine you are there, enjoying the results of your careful plans.

  - Now imagine you are planning a large wedding – perhaps a big celebration, like a Greek or Indian wedding, or perhaps a celebrity wedding, with high profile guests in an exotic location. Imagine all the steps you might go through to stage the event, from preparing the guest list to hiring dancers and arranging for flowers. Imagine the different travel arrangements needed to get everyone there. Imagine the lavish spread of food and entertainment you have planned. In short, go all out in your mind to make this an exciting gala event.

- Imagine you are making plans for a hiking or camping trip for several days in a beautiful wilderness location. Think about all the things you have to do to get ready, such as deciding where you are going to go, who you are going with, and what gear to take on the trip. Imagine the menu and the food you will bring with you. Or if you plan to hunt and fish, imagine getting that equipment together and imagine your route through the wilderness. If you plan a party before you leave, think about the plans for that, too. Finally, imagine you are on that trip, enjoying a great time as a result of your careful planning.

- Plan a vacation or trip you would like to take. Begin by deciding where you want to go and where to stop at along the way. Then, think about what you want to do when you get there, from sightseeing and going to markets to visiting fairs and art exhibits. Perhaps plan some gatherings with friends or think about a special occasion you want to attend, such as a big wedding or relative's graduation. Then, imagine yourself getting any clothes or equipment, such as a video camera or fishing gear, obtaining needed tickets and passports, and packing for the occasion. Finally, experience going on this great vacation or trip you have planned.

- Plan what you might do and say for an important upcoming event, such as going for a job interview, making a presentation to a client, or giving a speech. First, think about your objective or goal, so you have a general idea of what you want to say. Then, think more specifically about what to say, as if you are creating bullet points for a PowerPoint presentation. For each item you have created, imagine yourself saying or doing these things and practice these steps over and over in your mind. You'll find you'll get better and better, and this approach will help you make a great impression whatever you want to do.

• Imagine that you are planning a big party or community event. You might have a band, a host, great food, a theme, unique decorations, dozens or hundreds of attendees, and more. Imagine what you have to do to make the event happen. Start by deciding when it will be, where, and choose a theme. Think about who you want to invite and how to invite them. Think about the entertainment and who will host this. Decide on the type of food to serve and who will prepare and serve it. In short, imagine everything you have to do to make this gala event happen and imagine it going off without a hitch. Finally, you're there, having a great time. Besides being fun to plan the event, this exercise will help you better plan anything, as well as organize a real event.

CHAPTER 13: REMEMBER THIS

- Try to remember what you did earlier today, yesterday, or this past week. What did you do? What did you watch on TV? What did you read about in the newspaper or on the Internet? This is a great exercise for stretching your memory.

- Imagine you are creating a resume, in which you have to list all the jobs or experiences you had that would be relevant to the type of work you are seeking now. Think back to your most recent job or experience and remember the highlights and when these occurred. Then, go back to the next most recent job or experience. Or start with your first relevant job or experience after high school or college and go forward. However you start the process, try going backward and forward, like you are walking up and down steps and seeing a job or experience posted along the steps in chronological or reverse chronological order. By remembering, you will bring these experiences into your everyday consciousness, which will help you when you later look for work and someone asks you to describe how your past experiences will make you the ideal person to do the new job or assignment.

- Try to remember all the films you saw in the past week or month? Or list your top 10 films.

- Create a mental list of your top 10 favorite songs.

- Think back to your childhood and see how far back you can remember. Then, seek to recreate that event in your mind.

- Remember back to the firsts in your life. What was your first birthday party like? Your first date? Your first kiss?

- Experiment with observing some thing, place, or person and remembering as much detail as you can about what you observe. Then, test yourself by looking back to see how much you remembered. See how well you do if you have 5, 10, 15, or 20 seconds to observe. If you are driving, this is an ideal exercise to limber up your memory while on a rest break; otherwise, do this while sitting or waiting someplace. To test yourself, make a note of all the things you remember about what you saw; then look back and check yourself. Score a point for each thing you remember correctly, subtract a point for each thing you got wrong. Then, total the results. You'll find that you'll be able to remember more detail and remember it correctly, as you repeat this technique, so you'll see and remember things more precisely, wherever you are.

- Try to remember the names of all the roads you pass as you drive or walk somewhere you have never been before for 5 to 15 minutes. Allow more time if the roads are spaced further apart; less time if they are closer together. After the time is up, recite the names aloud or jot them down, and later you can check a map to see how many you got correct. . Score a point for each name you remember correctly, subtract a point for each name you got wrong or in the wrong order, and total the results. As with the other memory exercises, you'll be able to remember more detail correctly as you practice with this technique – and this improved memory will help you remember other things better, too.

CHAPTER 14: DECISIONS, DECISIONS

- If you have to make a decision in your life or work, reflect on what to do. Consider different possibilities and scenarios. Then, choose the one that feels right for you.

- Think about decisions you have made in the past and imagine what might have happened if you made a different decision.

- Suppose you have to decide about taking on a job or new project. Should you do it? Or is there something you would rather do? To help you decide, ask yourself about the pros and cons of taking that job or project? Which are stronger – the pros and the cons? You might think of them as two teams of players battling it out in your mind. Who is likely to win? Who do you want to win? Imagine the team you think is likely to win and the one you want to win becoming victorious, and you feel really good. That is the decision to make. What if the teams aren't the same, so you think one team or alternative is more likely, while you favor the other team or alternative? Then, notice how you feel in the two situations. Do you feel accepting of the more likely alternative, or do you want to fight it to help the team you prefer win? Whatever your choice, thinking of the different outcomes and how you feel about them will help you decide what to do.

- What if you lose your job or clients in your current field, because the industry is changing, so you aren't sure if you can get the same work in the future? What should you do next? One way to decide is to think about what skills you have. If you are going to remake yourself, how are you going to do it? What skills do you have that will be the most useful? A good way to think of possible outcomes is to consider what the market is looking for now or in the near future. Ask yourself what skills do you have and where do you think there might be a good match? Think about how your priorities for what you would rather do match up with what the market is interested in people doing now, assuming you have or can develop the skills to do this. Going over these possibilities in your mind will help you decide what to do next.

- Suppose you aren't sure what to do about a relationship, because you are having some problems? You can reflect on the pros and cons of the relationship and talk them out mentally or into a recorder. Think of the pros and cons of fixing what's wrong and keeping the relationship going or ending it and going on to something new. Again, you might imagine two teams battling it out – the pros and the cons, as you list the strengths and weaknesses of each team. In this case, you might not be sure who to root for, so watch as a neutral observer or judge as the teams battle it out. Notice which team seems to have the better or stronger arguments, the pros or the cons. Then, see one of the teams score a victory, and notice how you feel – relieved, sad, determined. Or maybe there could be a tie, so no one wins. In this case, take some time to think about the situation some more and schedule a rematch after you have more information or have some time to see the situation play out in real life, so you are in a better position to decide what to do.

CHAPTER 15: PLAYING FAVORITES

- Create some top 10 lists and think of 10 things to go on each list as quickly as possible, such as your 10 favorite movies, 10 famous quotes, or 10 funny things to say if I met the President of the U.S. on my next stop.

- Imagine you are doing your 10 favorite things, starting with #10 and working your way up.

- Think of a favorite word or saying. Imagine you are trying to tell someone else what this is using only pantomime and no words, as if you are playing charades. Imagine how you might convey the word or saying.

- Think of your favorite color. Imagine you have a paintbrush and are painting the scene in front of you with that color. For example, say your favorite color is red. Imagine that the clouds, trees, and fields are now red. Or maybe selectively paint things in that color, so, for example, you paint one tree red. Then, think of your least favorite color, and imagine painting things you don't like with that color, such as a nosey neighbor, prying co-worker, or tyrant boss.

- Think about why something is your favorite. Pick any favorite – a painting, book, song, saying, person, whatever. Think back to when that became a favorite and why; then enjoy thinking about that favorite thing. Try this exercise for different favorites. Finally, see all of your favorites lined up like honored objects on a shelf or onstage in a place of honor and enjoy seeing and remembering them again.

- Create a story about your favorites. To begin, think of three to five of your favorite things. Then, imagine a story where you incorporate all of them, much like when you have to use certain words in a story. For example, say your favorites are the book *Don Quixote*, because you love the unusual journey, the song: "Over the Rainbow," because you find it uplifting; the sport: "Tennis," because you enjoy the quick back and forth; the animal: the "panther," because it is sleek and crafty; and the vacation spot: the "mountains," because they are so majestic and beautiful. You might begin a story where Don Quixote is going on a quest to find the end of the rainbow so he can climb it, and along the way, he meets a panther who invites him to play a game of tennis high at his castle in the mountains, and once there he will reveal the secret of how to find a treasure that's over the rainbow. Try creating a story with three or four favorites, if you find it hard to link five favorites together; or combine more favorites into a story for an even greater challenge.

- Try any of the above exercises with your least favorite things. For example, make a list of your 10 least favorite things; remember when something became your least favorite thing or activity; imagine you are painting with your least favorite color; imagine you are creating a story with five of your least favorite things. Often you will find it funny when you engage in these activities – or treat them with a sense of humor. For example, create a story where things go horribly – and humorously – wrong. Or imagine yourself throwing darts or yelling out "raspberries" to whatever you don't like. The process is a little like creating a piñata with all the things you don't like, and then bursting it, so they scatter in the air. Or try throwing paintballs or darts at a target featuring your least favorite things.

CHAPTER 16: PRACTICE MAKES PERFECT

- Practice some skill in your mind and see yourself doing it very well – a technique which helps you perform the skill even better. You can work with a skill you already have or one you would like to learn. For example, see yourself practicing a sport, giving a speech, acting a part, participating in a job interview.

- Imagine yourself giving a speech in your mind. See yourself as an actor, politician, salesperson, or in any kind of job where you have to give presentations or performances.

- Imagine you are doing an interview to get some work you really want to do. Think of the major points you want to make during the interview to present yourself in the best light. Imagine you are at the interview, showing why you should get the work and see yourself getting it. Practice doing this again and again to firm up your memory of doing a successful interview. Then, you will more easily and comfortably do the interview in the real situation.

- Imagine you are an attorney representing the prosecution or defense in a case you have read about in the news. Come up with some arguments you might make to support your case, and practice giving those arguments in your mind or speak them aloud. You'll become better and better as you practice and you'll find this ability will carry over into making you more persuasive in your everyday life.

- Imagine you are participating in a sport you enjoy doing or watching. But now you are practicing to become a champion. Imagine yourself working out and getting better and better each time you practice. This kind of mental practice will also carry over into everyday life.

- Imagine you are an actor or actress in a film, and you are playing your role in a big scene. People are gathered around watching, the cameras are rolling, and the director calls out "Action!" Then you perform your role – again and again – in a series of takes, getting better each time.

CHAPTER 17: SOUND OFF

- Pay attention to the sounds around you. For example, as you drive, you might notice the wind rushing past your car. You might notice the sound of the road under your tires, and notice how it changes as you drive on a smooth paved surface and on a gravel surface, where you hear the whirring, crunching, gravelly sound. Or as you wait someplace, you might notice the clicking clock on the wall, the footsteps of people passing by, the whirr of a plane in the air, and the soft rustle of bushes in the distance.

- Experiment with listening to sounds in different directions. For example, focus your attention on the sounds in front of you, then the sounds on your right, then the sounds behind you, and next the sounds to your left. Afterwards repeat the process. As you get good at noticing sounds in different directions, try listening to the sounds spaced around you like the hands of a clock, listening first to those in the 12 noon or midnight position; then 1 a.m. or p.m., 2 a.m. or p.m., 3 a.m. or p.m., and so on; or reverse and listen in a counterclockwise direction. (The process is much like practicing looking in each direction and bringing your eyes back to center, but now you are paying attention to sounds.)

- Try speaking or singing aloud, though in a private place or with an agreeable group, when you do the following.

- Sing aloud as you listen to music – or make up your own songs and sing them. Do this individually or as a group sing.

- Make animals sounds, as you listen to music – individually or turn this into a chorus of different animals. Some popular suggestions: a dog, wolf, cat, chimpanzee, gorilla, parrot, hooting owl, and other types of birds.

- Imagine you are outside in the woods, mountains, park, zoo, or in your own backyard, and as you see different animals, make sounds for them. For example, think of different types of birds and make calls for them. Or make cat calls, wolf howls, dog barks, sheep bleats, and geese honks. Just have fun, and feel like a little kid as you make these different animal sounds.

- Imagine you are a horn and sound out as you pass different high points, such as the beginning of a lake or river, a towering tree, an exit sign along the road. Make your sounds even louder when you pass something especially interesting.

- Speak into a recording device – or imagine speaking into such a device – and report what you are seeing as you drive or observe the scene around you. For example, while driving, you might report on seeing cranes and pumps and describe what they are doing.

CHAPTER 18: MENTAL TRIPPING

- Imagine you are with someone you want to be with and are doing various activities together.

- Imagine this is a perfect day, and you are spending it doing whatever you want.

- Imagine you are taking a trip to a foreign country.

- Imagine you are going on a visit to the zoo.

- Imagine you are visiting someone – and project yourself there in your mind.

- Imagine you are flying high in the sky and looking down on whatever you pass.

- Imagine this is a day in the future, and imagine where you are and what you are doing.

- Imagine you are enjoying a day at the beach. You are lying on the sand, swimming in the ocean, surfing the waves – do whatever you want to do.

- Imagine you are hiking in the woods or mountains. See yourself on the trail, as you pass beautiful hills and valleys, walk by creeks, see flowers, and listen to birds and other animal sounds.

- Imagine you are looking up at the clouds, and you see shapes of people and animals form there. Then, as the clouds move and break up, you see these shapes dissolve and form into other shapes.

- Imagine you are skating on the ice in a lake or outdoor rink with other skaters. You feel exhilarated as you skate and feel the sense of freedom, as you move quickly along the ice and feel the wind in your hair.

- Imagine you are sailing on a boat in a lake or on a ship on the ocean on a beautiful sunny day. Imagine you are on deck observing the water as you travel. You notice the waves going up and down, schools of fish passing by, and you feel very calm and peaceful.

- Imagine you are taking a trip into outer space in a rocket ship. You see stars and planets as you travel, and when you look back, you see earth becoming smaller and smaller as you speed ahead. Then, you feel yourself floating, free of the pull of earth's gravity, and you enjoy the sense of moving freely, like a balloon.

- Imagine yourself as a balloon – or in a balloon – floating over the countryside. You feel the wind around you, moving you along, and as you look down, you see everything glide by like in a dream.

- Imagine you are in a magical kingdom where you are a king or queen, and as you travel around visiting your lands, you are adored by your subjects who cheer you on.

- Imagine you are on an archaeological adventure trip, where you are exploring ancient ruins from a long-buried civilization. You see the ruins of old temples, houses, marketplaces, carvings, and paintings on the wall.

- Imagine you are going anywhere you want and doing anything you want there, for in mental tripping you can create your own trip wherever you want and with whomever you want in your mind.

CHAPTER 19: LEARN A LITTLE

- Play some educational tapes, CDs, or mobile apps. Beyond listening, form questions in your mind and answer them, and you'll learn even more.

- Play a tape, CD, or mobile app of a book, and actively visualize the story as you drive or wait for something.

  - If it's non-fiction, reflect on what the narrator has said.

  - If it's fiction, imagine yourself as one of the main characters.

  - Or imagine yourself as a member of an audience listening to a speaker and ask questions and imagine what the speaker says in response.

- Stop at a visitor's center, and look at the displays or films. Then, while still there or when you drive on, reflect on what you have seen. Ask questions in your mind to help you remember what you learned. Or imagine what it was like if you lived in the time or place shown in the photos or films. For instance, say you stop at a visitor center devoted to the Ohlone Indians who lived along the coast of Northern California. You might imagine what life might be like if you were an Ohlone Indian. You might see yourself living in one of the small houses made of bark and reeds. You might imagine yourself at a ceremony. You might imagine hunting for game or gathering plants for food. Whatever you have learned, use your imagination to make it seem more real and memorable. Later, you can apply this visualization technique to better learning and remembering anything by making it more dramatic and real, and therefore more a part of you.

CHAPTER 20: KEEP ON TRIPPING

Now that you've got the idea, come up with more ideas and ways to have more fun while you're traveling or waiting for something to happen. That's what I did with many of these ideas – I thought them up and then tried them out, which really made my time driving or waiting really fly.

Think of the process like making anything. Essentially, whatever you observe or experience is like your raw materials. Then, you apply your imagination and creativity to your observations or experience to dramatize them, heighten the experience, and make them come alive for you. You'll experience all kinds of positive results – from having fun to helping you relax, stimulating your mental abilities, increasing your creativity, and coming up with ideas you can turn into a creative project, product, or profitable enterprise.

The possibilities are endless. So keep on tripping and turn driving or waiting time into an explosion of fun, creative, relaxing, enjoyable, and productive ideas.